Affect and Emotion

Graham Music

Series editor: Ivan Ward

ICON BOOKS UK

TOTEM BOOKS USA

Published in the UK in 2001
by Icon Books Ltd., Grange Road,
Duxford, Cambridge CB2 4QF
E-mail: info@iconbooks.co.uk
www.iconbooks.co.uk

Published in the USA in 2001
by Totem Books
Inquiries to: Icon Books Ltd.,
Grange Road, Duxford
Cambridge CB2 4QF, UK

Sold in the UK, Europe, South Africa
and Asia by Faber and Faber Ltd.,
3 Queen Square, London WC1N 3AU
or their agents

Distributed to the trade in the USA
by National Book Network Inc.,
4720 Boston Way, Lanham,
Maryland 20706

Distributed in the UK, Europe,
South Africa and Asia by
Macmillan Distribution Ltd.,
Houndmills, Basingstoke RG21 6XS

Distributed in Canada by
Penguin Books Canada,
10 Alcorn Avenue, Suite 300,
Toronto, Ontario M4V 3B2

Published in Australia in 2001
by Allen & Unwin Pty. Ltd.,
PO Box 8500, 83 Alexander Street,
Crows Nest, NSW 2065

ISBN 1 84046 243 4

Text copyright © 2001 Graham Music

The author has asserted his moral rights.

Series editor: Ivan Ward

Typesetting by Hands Fotoset

Printed and bound in the UK by
Cox & Wyman Ltd., Reading

Introduction

How strange that all
The errors, pains, and early miseries,
Regrets, vexations, lassitudes interfused
Within my mind, should e'er have borne a part,
And that a needful part, in making up
The calm existence that is mine when I
Am worthy of myself.[1]

(Wordsworth)

In this essay, I look at emotions or *affects* from a psychoanalytic perspective. *Emotionality* is absolutely central to the psychoanalytic enterprise, as it is to all human experience. What distinguishes a psychoanalytic 'take' on the world of feelings and emotions is the idea that we are all in varying degrees unaware or unconscious of aspects of what we are feeling. Psychoanalytic practice aims both to help people become more aware of their emotional functioning, and to develop a greater capacity to tolerate and manage a wider range of emotional experience. These are twin threads that run throughout this essay.

3

The concepts 'feeling', 'emotion' and 'affect' have similar meanings, and psychoanalytic and ordinary dictionaries tend to define one in relation to the others. 'Affect' is a less widely used concept, seen mainly in the domains of academic psychology and theoretical psychoanalytic works, and it tends to have a more objective feel, of something that can be *observed* rather than *experienced*. Its use fits with the traditional distrust of subjective experience in academia, where until recently, even in neuroscience, emotion was not seen as an area fit for study. 'Feeling', on the other hand, denotes an *internal* state, someone's private experience. One cannot observe a feeling but one can observe the effect of a feeling or see signs of someone's feelings. 'Emotion' is the ordinary language equivalent of 'affect', having a more objective quality than 'feelings'. We talk about observing an emotional response in someone, and some have argued that the site of an emotion is the body, whereas the site of a feeling is the mind. Yet people also talk of both 'emotional' and 'affective' experience, and given the blurring of the boundaries

4

between these concepts, for my purposes the concepts will be used fairly interchangeably, despite this being something of a simplification.[2]

There is something artificial about separating out affect or emotion from other aspects of mental life such as cognition or memory. Indeed, when Freud originally wrote about repressed memories of childhood sexual abuse he described how memories of traumatic events are closely linked with feelings. He believed early in his career that if one were able to discharge the emotions associated with particular memories then these memories would lose their power to haunt. The separation between the cognitive and the emotional is not absolute. For example, I noticed in myself that when watching a film recently I was reminded of an old friend, then felt sad at the passing time, then I remembered a book we had discussed and this led to me thinking about a forthcoming event, and I found myself feeling anxious and excited, and then I remembered a dream and almost instantly I thought about an unfinished job and so on, this all maybe lasting but a few seconds. Such trains of associations are one reason why psychoanalysis has used the technique of 'free association', in which patients are encouraged to say whatever comes into their head. Associations activate other associations, so that, for example, thinking about the time passed since last seeing my friend reminded me of time passing generally, and then other thoughts popped up. Feelings are a bewildering mixture, both evanescent and yet central to our beings, or as John Updike wrote: '[Its] funny about feelings, they seem to come and go in a flash, yet outlast metal.'[3]

We now know that the parts of the brain involved in emotional experience are different from other parts of the brain. People can suffer damage to the left hemisphere to such an extent that they do not recognise their own spouses or even know their names, but often such patients still act towards their spouses appropriately, and this is because another type of learning takes place elsewhere in the brain where the emotional centres lie. A patient of Anthony Damasio had very localised damage to her brain, in fact a calcified amygdala. She could not feel fear, whereas her other emotions such as anger were functioning ordinarily. As a result this patient was overly trusting, and unable to learn from bad experiences, as she did not receive the warning signs that fear enables.[4] Such brain damage affects people's emotional capacities. There is now much evidence, though, that things can go in the opposite direction and that severe emotional factors, such as trauma, result in changed brain structure. Susan Greenfield, for example, described a Vietnam veteran whose hippocampus was enlarged following traumatic wartime experiences.[5] Rather than arguing that the brain is primary and affects our emotions, or vice versa, in chicken-and-egg type debate, it seems more sensible to acknowledge that brain-states and emotional experiences are two sides of the same coin.

Some have doubted the usefulness of the concept of the *unconscious*, but there has been an increasing body of research, both psychological and neuroscientific, to back up the idea of unconscious emotional states. For example, a sample of the group of people who tend to have what are called 'avoidant attachment patterns' were subjected to an experiment.[6] Such people tend to dismiss the importance of relationships and intimacy, and to deny the meaningfulness of separations, whether in their current life or in the past. Yet this same group were asked in experiments to recall memories of separation, rejection and threat involving their parents. The results showed that the more the subjects used 'avoidant' strategies and denied to themselves or others any difficulties, the stronger the physiological reactions they had, such as increased perspiration and a quickened pulse rate. Other experiments have yielded similar results, including those monitoring emotional parts of the brain. In this essay, I examine how people cope or do not cope with the different challenges of an emotional life, how emotions can be, for example, denied, clung to, feared, used defensively, got rid of, or converted into illness, and what psychoanalysis might have to say about the kinds of challenges that are thrown up by our emotionality.

Urges and Instincts

Freud wrote only a little about emotions and affects. However, a concept that was central to his thinking was that of the 'drives'. By this he meant something akin to instincts and urges. Affects or emotions such as anger or rage were considered by Freud and many of his contemporaries to be linked with an aggressive drive. There was a different conception of human nature when Freud was writing, from around the end of the 19th century. Then, supposedly 'base' traits, such as untrammelled sexual urges and aggressive self-interest, were often considered to be primary instinctual drives that needed to be 'civilised out' if not kept at bay, or banished to the unconscious. For example, finding the spouse of a friend attractive and wishing to act upon this might be something that we feel, but are ashamed of and do not want to feel. We might try to get rid of this feeling somehow, and the moral part of the mind, what Freud called the 'superego', might censor this illicit desire. The illicit desire might then be said to exist and yet one might not know about it, or at least might both

9

'know' unconsciously and simultaneously have no conscious awareness of it.

Sian had been to the opening of her new exhibition with her family. Her eldest daughter is now 17 and looked particularly stunning that night and received compliment after compliment. Sian was proud of her daughter but still noticed a twinge of jealousy, feeling that the days when she would have received such accolades were long gone. She could not quite enjoy what was supposed to be her night, forcing herself into her role as hostess, and being nicer than usual to her daughter. It was only when chatting to friends later in the week that Sian could, with tremendous relief and even humour, own up to these feelings.

Psychoanalysis has often been associated with a radical challenge to contemporary values and morals. Cultural icons such as Elvis Presley in the 1950s or the Sex Pistols in the 1970s were feared by some and championed by others for endorsing the rebellious, sexual and aggressive attitudes that mainstream culture denied. Many early psycho-analysts such as Wilhelm Reich supported revolutionary sexual, political and educational ideas. Facing the unconscious is by no means simply about controlling it, but often about daring to be surprised by it and embracing what we might otherwise deny. Psychoanalysis is maybe less about *knowing* one's unconscious than about *respecting* its awesomeness, as H. L. Mencken suggests in this quote:

Penetrating so many secrets
we cease to believe in the unknowable
But there it sits nevertheless
calmly licking its chops.[7]

Sian's jealousy was natural and understandable given the circumstances. Yet some people steadfastly deny ever experiencing such emotions, fearing they are socially unacceptable. It is easy to feel critical of such feelings in others and ashamed of them in ourselves. Indeed, Sian probably attempted such an evasion initially when she found herself being nicer than usual to her daughter, as an attempt to spare both herself and her daughter from her true feelings. Such a ploy, often done unconsciously, is an example of what Freud called a 'reaction formation' – an attempt to deny one's true emotional state by taking on the opposite affect. We might see this in people who are said to 'protest too much', as Shakespeare pointed out so long ago, and in Emerson's example: 'the louder he talked of his honor the faster we counted our spoons'.[8] Jealousy is an example of an emotion that many of us wish we did not feel, and so fits the description of the unacceptable feelings, urges, drives and emotions of which Freud wrote.

Sian's feelings were understandable, meaning both that we might be sympathetic to her plight, and also that her feelings may have a meaning that we can make sense of. This links to another view of emotion in which such feelings can be taken as signs to be read, as a form of communication from one part of the self to another. 'Signal anxiety' was the concept used to describe this in Freud's time, and is still in use. If one is in a social situation and one's heart suddenly starts beating fast, one can take this as a sign of something. For example, a young man *Stephen* was at a party and trying to be nice to someone when he realised that his fists were clenching and the muscles around his neck were tightening. It was only upon noticing this 'signal' that he realised that he had been feeling uneasy about being pressurised by the person he was talking to. Possibly in my earlier example, Sian's feelings about her daughter were a message to her. She had not managed to face painful feelings about the loss of her youth and a move into middle age. Banishing the feelings as opposed to daring to face them had been counter-productive, not allowing her to begin to confront what it meant to be embarking on the next phase of her life.

So, some emotional responses can be a sign whose coded language we may be lucky enough to decipher. Yet other feelings seem more like an alien presence that has shockingly invaded us. This sense of 'otherness', of feelings being 'out of character', might be similar to Freud's conception of instinctual drives over which we feel that we have no power. Indeed, psychoanalysis has taught us to respect the surprises that may be sprung upon us by the unconscious. Stephen, the young man at the party, had recently been given the 'brush-off' by a former girlfriend and had been aggressive and threatening in response. Afterwards he was shocked at himself and said, 'It was not like me'.

Such internal conflicts were Stephen's lot. As a bright 16-year-old who was struggling to manage adolescence, he had found himself confronted by major bodily and hormonal changes. Adolescence, and the earlier onset of puberty, had been a huge shock, leaving him feeling assailed by a whole new array of emotional states. He might swiftly move from having powerful sexual fantasies at one moment to feeling superior and grandiose the next, and lurch from falling in love to feeling desperately needy and all at sea, as if he was suddenly catapulted onto an emotional roller-coaster over which he had no control. I am reminded of the lines from *Richard III*:

What myself upon myself?
Alack I love myself. Wherefore?
Oh no. Alas, I rather hate myself

For hateful deeds committed by myself!
I am a villain; yet I lie, I am not.[9]

It is controversial within psychoanalysis whether it is still helpful to think in terms of drives, but certainly young people like Stephen are confronted by hormonally-led affective states that they can barely manage. People often wish that such feelings would be made to go away. Ironically, one often finds that the psychotherapist might be more inclined to help people accept, manage or integrate these frightening emotional states rather than help to get rid of them. An Ancient Rabbi, Israel of Rizhyn, is reported to have said that God created man as he is 'not to be caged by his lusts but to be *free in them*'.[10]

Managing Loss

Mourning was one of the first areas of emotional experience that psychoanalysis grappled with. Freud wrote that the effect of a profound loss in our lives can seem similar to what he then called *melancholia* and is now normally referred to as *depression*. Both in depression and bereavement, the person may withdraw into their own world, seem lacklustre, be self-critical, seem morbidly preoccupied with events in the past and exhibit other similar symptoms. Freud argued that we might consider someone who is bereaved to be 'ill' if we did not know the cause of their behaviour. Loss can be managed in different ways. As a Hassidic sage said:

There are two kinds of sorrow . . . When a man broods over the misfortunes that have come upon him, when he cowers in a corner and despairs of help, that is a bad kind of sorrow . . . The other kind of sorrow is the honest grief of a man whose house has burned down, who feels his need deep in his soul and begins to build anew.[11]

Marion, a 45-year-old mother of three, had been married to Peter for 18 years when he suddenly died of a heart attack. Marion was, at first, in a state of utter shock and numbness. She could not take in the awful truth of what had happened, and for a long time she just could not believe it. She would prepare Peter's evening meal as usual, forgetting the unbearable reality of his death. Later she also felt terribly guilty and wondered what she could have done to prevent his death. She also found herself feeling absolutely furious with Peter. 'Why did he have to work so hard?', she would ask, and exclaim: 'How selfish to leave us like this.' She felt ashamed of such feelings, though they are only too common under the circumstances. Her feelings would ebb and flow, as she moved in and out of numbed disbelief, irrational clinging to the past, a furious rage with Peter and others, and a dreadful heart-rending pain. For a long time Marion seemed to be in her own world, barely available to her children who needed her as never before. Those who have suffered tragic life-events such as this may take a very long time to even begin to recover. Vera Brittain wrote poignantly of her grief over the death of her lover:

... time, they told me, with maddening uniformity, would heal. I resented the suggestion bitterly ...

17

clinging assiduously to my pain I did not know then
that if the living are to be of any use in this world,
they must always break faith with the dead.[12]

It is a long painful journey to work through such losses and to find a way to move back into life, hopefully with a sense of gratitude for what one has gained from the lost loved one. Such huge losses continue to be worked through, and reverberate, for the rest of one's life.

Some do not manage to work through such life-events. An example from literature is Miss Havisham in Dickens's *Great Expectations* (1860–1). She was jilted on her wedding day, and lived until old age stuck in a time warp, surrounded externally by a decaying wedding cake and a clock stopped at the hour of her betrayal, as if time could be stopped at that dreadful moment. Internally she was as eaten up as her mice-ridden wedding cake, full of hatred and bitterness and fantasies of revenge. She is a stark example of someone who has not been able to work through the painful process of mourning and slowly move back into life.

Throughout life we all face losses of varying proportions, from giving up the breast as an infant to the death of pets, to life-changes such as leaving school or moving home. Some manage such losses better than others. In the last section we met Sian, whom we saw struggling with her daughter's move into womanhood and her own transition to middle age. The move to middle age marks one kind of loss, signalling the end of youth and a step nearer to death. These are painful things to confront and face, and some 'cope' by denial. Others desperately attempt to stave off an unwanted reality by rushing headlong into frenetic activity, overworking, having affairs, or aping youthful fashions and lifestyles. The school leaver who scornfully denigrates his younger former school fellows and rushes frantically into late night parties and drinking may be trying to ward off painful feelings about the loss of the safe and known, of helpful adult figures and cherished friends. The man who 'copes' with middle age, or rather struggles against it, by buying sports cars or having affairs exemplifies a wish to deny the brutal facts of mortality and a failing body. Feelings such as excitement, elation or triumph experienced in such circumstances are all real feelings, but are feelings that can arise in an attempt to ward off or defend against other more painful feelings. One affective state can be used to deny another.

Psychoanalysis has traditionally argued that the painful in life cannot be evaded without cost, but needs to be faced, and that life becomes the richer for doing so. As Thomas Hardy wrote:

. . . if way to the better be, it exacts a full look at the worst.[13]

There can be tremendous relief when difficult feelings are managed and not fled, such as when the angry frantic child whose beloved grandmother has died breaks down at last and lets out the grief everyone but them knew was inside.

Hopefully at times we can manage to tolerate and face unpleasant realities. Most contemporary psychoanalytic theorists would say that people are aided by something inside themselves, an internal capacity that helps to process emotional experience. This capacity is often viewed as something alive inside the mind – a friendly figure, often called a 'good internal object' – that can offer help when needed.[14] Others are less lucky. Sometimes such psychological capacities are present but have been damaged, but in others they may never have developed, either as a result of their genetic predisposition or because they were never lucky enough to have their emotional lives taken seriously during their formative years. In such cases, the job of the psychoanalytic therapist is not just that of the bereavement counsellor, allowing the natural process of grief or mourning to unfold. Rather, it can be more like being with a young child or infant, and sympathetically and painstakingly helping them to develop the rudiments of experiencing and tolerating an emotional life.

Early Experience and Emotional States

. . . do you know who made you? 'Nobody knows as

*I know on' said the child with a short laugh . . . 'I
'spect I growed'.*[15]

(Harriet Beecher Stowe)

It has become a truism to say that one's emotional
self is influenced by one's early life. In recent
decades, huge bodies of research have emerged in
related fields – such as developmental psychology,
neuroscience, attachment theory and the psychoanalytic observation of infants, amongst many
others – which stress the impact of early
experiences on development, including emotional
development. Sylvia Plath in a poem to her
daughter described her as: 'A clean slate, with your
own face on.'[16] Genetic endowment is important,
and its role relative to that of nurture is controversial, but nonetheless, few now doubt the
importance of early experiences.

Humans are born with distinct and genetically
determined predispositions, but how these become
patterns of experiencing the world for particular
individuals is more complicated. Many studies
have illustrated that even within the womb learn-

ing is taking place, and infants have been shown to remember not just particular voices, such as those of their parents, but also to exhibit clear preferences after birth for specific stories or pieces of music they had heard in the womb.[17] While it is true that many emotional capacities are already formed in the early months of infancy, the infant is still barely a person, and depends almost entirely on its mother or primary caretaker for its physical and emotional needs. The infant is born with a brain and nervous system that can regulate important physiological functions such as body temperature and heartbeat. However, the capacity to regulate emotional states is a later development. Before this ability develops, the infant needs an external regulator of its emotions, normally the mother or other caretaker.

The infant in distress needs not only soothing but also to know that its feelings are understood and that someone is making sense of their experience for them. An 8-month-old baby *Robert* started wailing when for the first time he heard the loud sound of the spin-dryer going at full throttle.

His mother at first was anxious and worried, wondering what had caused the upset, and had to grapple with her own response to her infant's distress. Soon she realised what had happened, picked him up and began to carry him around, tenderly letting him know that he was alright. She then went back to the machine, turning it off and on again several times while talking about what was going on. The words may have made little sense, but the emotional meaning was transmitted through the basic tone and rhythm of her speech. In no time Robert had recovered, and the object of terror had become an object of interest, one which he soon wanted to turn on and off by himself.

In this brief interaction, the mother functioned as a kind of emotional 'shield' for Robert, helping him to manage his own feelings and interpreting the world for him. Many psychotherapists use the model of mother–infant interactions to aid them in their practice, partly because what people need help with emotionally often has parallels with these very early processes. Psychotherapists have to make sense of feelings in their patients, and often also need first to explore their own feelings and what a patient might stir up in them. Infants similarly need another person to modulate their experience of the world. Some infants, like some adults, are hypersensitive to external stimuli, and easily shocked by the kind of sudden noises just mentioned. Such hypersensitivity can make being a parent far harder and requires special input, but nonetheless all infants are profoundly affected by the quality of early care they receive.

Infants' capacities are often underestimated. It is known that an infant needs only to experience something twice for an expectation to develop of the same thing happening again under similar circumstances. The infant, whose cries are ignored or even punished, soon learns not to cry, or to cry without expecting a response. Infants of depressed mothers have been shown by 6 months to show depressed behaviour when with non-depressed adults. They soon learn to predict adult reactions and from early in life form expectations of how interactions are likely to go. These become what have been variously called 'internal working models',[18] or 'schemas', or RIGS (Representations of Interactions Generalised).[19] Some describe these internal models of relationships as 'internal object relations', and most would see them as partly based on real experience and partly on how the mind interprets these experiences. These expectations can then become the basis for how we relate to the world. *Hilary*, a 35-year-old woman, developed an expectation as a child that she would be rejected if she got angry with her parents, and as an adult expected to be similarly rebuffed. In relationships, as eventually with a therapist, she was too nice and sugary, assuming that no one would bear her if she showed any disgruntlement. This is one example of what can be meant by 'transference' to someone else, a transfer of expectations into a current relationship from a prior one. Recognising such patterns, it is hoped, can lead to them changing.

Emotions and feelings are very much tied up with belief systems and thought structures, and cannot be separated from them. The child who at nursery was fiercely shouted at by a man with a red beard might well be fearful of other men with red beards, and might develop a belief, conscious or not, that men with red beards are dangerous. This is partly a behavioural response, rather like Pavlov's dogs salivating when they hear the bell that signifies food arriving. Much psychoanalytic thought has distanced itself from such ideas, seeing behavioural explanations and treatments as contrary to the focus of psychoanalysis on thought and insight. However, recently psychologists and others have tried to bring together an emphasis on behaviour with an emphasis on internal repre-sentations. Some use a distinction between two kinds of memories, sometimes called explicit and implicit memory, or 'declarative memory' as opposed to 'procedural memory'. An example of declarative or explicit memory would be remem-bering certain facts, such as a phone number or that one went to the hairdresser and left one's umbrella there. Procedural or implicit memory is of a different order, and relates to skills and capa-cities or the way we act. An example of procedural memory would be riding a bicycle, a skill one learns but then does seemingly naturally, no more consciously remembering how to do this than the centipede needs to think consciously about how it walks. These are deeply ingrained ways of being, which have cognitive, emotional and bodily components. The distinction between procedural and declarative memory is not an absolute one, but it is a useful shorthand for thinking about how our emotional lives can form into patterned procedures that repeat themselves over time. These patterns are laid down when we are very young, before much of the brain which processes complex cognitive skills has begun to develop.

For example, particular parts of our brains respond when we are having a positive emotional experience, and this can now be easily measured while it is happening. Recent research has shown to be the case what some have believed intuitively, that infants are profoundly influenced by the mood states of those around them.[20] Infants and children cannot help but respond positively in the presence of an adult who is smiling happily. This happens automatically, and the infant brain can be shown to respond accordingly. In other words, the infant's mood state, and indeed its brain activity, tend to mirror the mother's face. Such experiences develop into patterns of responding based on past experience. Other research has shown that the brains of children with seriously depressed mothers tend to be organised differently from the norm.

The 1990s were described by many as the 'decade of the brain', and much exciting new research published in the last few years has backed up ideas that are central to psychoanalysis. Neural pathways are the main means by which messages are carried to and from parts of the brain (although some are carried via the blood stream). Research shows that traumatised children tend to develop particular neuronal pathways, those giving rise to hypersensitivity and 'fight or flight' responses.[21] Such children become hyper-alert to danger, and sniff out potential warnings that others may never notice. It is as if their brains become 'hard-wired' to respond to tiny signals, which are interpreted as danger signs. The pathways associated with such responses are overdeveloped in these children, and other parts of the brain are underdeveloped. A huge amount of brain development occurs within the first few years of life, when the basis of one's personality is being formed. This is an argument for offering early help when necessary, as such patterns can be changed and even reversed with the right kind of help. The traumatised child may develop a 'super-highway' of neuronal pathways leading to anxiety and hyper-alertness, whereas luckier babies such as Robert will develop 'super-highways' to healthier emotional responses.

Templates of emotional experience that are seeded early often become the central focus in psychoanalytic therapy. Hilary, the 35-year-old woman mentioned above, entered therapy follow-ing a series of disastrous relationships in which she felt hurt and rejected, and from which she tended to flee. There were clear links with how mistreated she felt by partners and how she was genuinely mistreated as a child. Interestingly, she was soon mistrustful of her male therapist. At first she felt that she had to be nice and sweet, but underneath more difficult feelings were brewing. She felt that she was being used, that her feelings were ignored, that some of what he said was cruel and rejecting, and that if he cared he would see her more, charge less and be kinder. Such pivotal issues emerge in their full and shocking splendour during therapy where they need to be 'worked through'. Often this means both parties in a therapeutic or other relationship must experience what it is like to be inside an emotional interaction which they need both to understand and find their way out of. Hilary needed a therapist who could tolerate the position he was being placed in, and help to think about the patterns that were being re-enacted inside and outside the consulting room, such as when her view was right, and when she exaggerated or misread situations. This is a profoundly emotional process for both parties, and not simply about insight in any intellectual sense. Such repetitive patterns are based on procedural memories that have to be relived in order to be challenged.

Cut Off from Feelings

The body's life is the life of sensations and emotions. [22]

(D. H. Lawrence)

The human mind can inspire drastic but necessary methods of avoiding the unbearable. For example, a common response to terrible news is numbness or disbelief, and a traumatised person may cope by dissociating or going off into his or her own world. The abused girl may need to dispel thoughts about the injustice of her predicament by denying the awfulness of what she has experienced. Similarly, it might be foolhardy for the young boy who gets beaten when he complains to protest, as his protests only lead to further punishment, and in time such a child may ignore or forget his own need to protest. Few would deny the sensibleness of these ways of cutting oneself off from emotional experience, and indeed it is possible to be *too* in touch with painful situations. Perhaps this is why there is suspicion of the current vogue for dispatching busloads of counsellors to the after-math of traumatic events. There are times when it is not right to stare pain in the face and sometimes people need help to forget pain. As Brian Keenan wrote following his imprisonment and torture in Beirut, 'to drag a man into talking of something he has neither the desire nor the ability to discuss is a kind of selfish brutality'.[23]

However, psychoanalysis more often has been involved in thinking about and trying to help the opposite condition, those people who are suffer-ing because they are out of touch with their own emotional lives. *Marcia*, *James* and *Frank* were chatting in the pub when the conversation moved from relaxed discussion about work and holidays to thinking about how difficult it is being a parent these days. Frank mentioned how he remembers his own childhood, how his father was always away and how sometimes sad feelings well up inside when he is with his own young son. Marcia says that she feels the same, but also feels guilty that she just wants to get away from her children and cannot bear to spend too much time with them. James had been joining in before, but in response to strong feelings such as Frank's sadness he began to look awkward, started fidgeting and eventually got up to leave. We might wonder what was going on for James, who generally seems to head for an escape route when emotional matters are being discussed. One might say he is 'threatened' by such matters, or 'cannot handle them', or that he 'avoids' the emotional world and a feeling in part of himself of which he is possibly not conscious.

A masculinity based on being tough and unfeeling has been glorified in our culture, as can be seen when Clint Eastwood is cast as the heroic deadpan hard man of few words. In the films *High Plains Drifter* and *Pale Rider*, he plays supernatural characters returned from the dead, 'literally non-human', and hence non-feeling. In *Hang 'Em High*, a sheriff tells him to go to hell and he replies 'I've already been there'.[24] This is an idealisation of a tough, thick-skinned and uncommunicative person whose emotions are deliberately locked well away. James' veneer though was less tough

34

than this, and he lacked Eastwood's laconic confidence. He had little capacity to know his own emotional experience. He had had a troubled adolescence, including a period of anorexia. Yet at the time he did not feel that anything was wrong, and in fact appeared not to know what others meant when they used emotional words like 'sad' or 'annoyed'. Children and adults who are diagnosed as *autistic* often exhibit a similar lack of understanding of the world of feelings. Some other people are able to manage particular feelings but baulk at the rest, and so might be only too quick to let other people (and themselves) know when they are happy, but cannot quite admit when they are sad. Still others have a finely-honed sensibility to the world of emotions, differentiating the subtlest nuances between affective states such as anger, irritation, annoyance, or what the difference might be between feeling 'peeved' as opposed to 'ratty' as opposed to 'uptight' or 'shirty' or 'livid' or 'rankled' or 'vexed', for example.

This is partly cultural. Eskimos are said to have

numerous different words for snow and so actually experience snow differently to us. Other cultures lack, for example, a conception of guilt as opposed to shame and so cannot be said to experience what we might call guilt. Our language frames our experiences of the world. As Eva Hoffman wrote:

Sometimes, when I find a new expression, I roll it on the tongue, as if shaping it in my mouth gave birth to a new shape in the world.[25]

Each family too might be said to have its own emotional culture. In some families rage is frowned upon but sadness is allowed, or in others worry is more acceptable than exuberance. Someone growing up in a home where jealousy was stigmatised might work hard to avoid jealousy, or at least to disguise this feeling from themselves or others. Such a person might be seen to slam the door a little too loudly when their spouse is talking to someone else, but might not actually know that they are jealous, or, in other words, they might not be able to experience their own hidden feelings of jealousy.

James, the man mentioned above who beat a hasty retreat from his friends' emotional conversation, is typical of certain people who feel profoundly uncomfortable when in contact with emotions in themselves or others. The caricature of a man who spends all his time on his computer or the female academic who immerses herself in the world of books and the intellect, and who both struggle to manage real relationships, are examples of this predicament. Psychoanalysis has traditionally thought of these people as 'defending against' emotions, which are 'repressed' or 'disowned'. We all know of times when we might reach for a newspaper, cigarette, chocolate bar or some other distraction rather than face some unsettling emotion. Yet there are also examples of people who are not defending against feelings, but rather do not have the capacity as yet to experience their own emotional states.

Earlier I mentioned how emotions can function as signs or signals from one part of the self to another. A person walking down a street who sees someone they are attracted to and whose heart starts racing might only then realise how they feel about this person. Others could not make this connection at all. In experiments with infants aged about one year, their mothers are asked to suddenly leave the room. In response, some infants cry and get very upset, whereas others barely seem to react and carry on as if nothing has happened. These latter children, often labelled 'avoidantly attached', also seem not to notice when their mothers return, whereas the 'securely attached' infants rush to their mothers for comfort. Yet, when the pulse rate, adrenalin and cortisol levels of both groups are measured, we see that all have similar physiological reactions to their mothers' disappearance. One would not know this from ordinary observation, and clearly the avoidant group is not as 'in touch' with their feelings.[26] Interestingly, it is this group which a huge body of research has begun to prove are far more likely to grow up less emotionally literate, less able to talk about feelings and less likely to form loving, physically and emotionally close bonds.

There are adults who function perfectly well in

this way and seem to live perfectly normal lives, so normal that their lives seem to the outsider to be emotionally shallow, lacking in all depth. The psychoanalyst Joyce McDougall coined the term 'robotic' for such people,[27] and another, Christopher Bollas, wrote of 'normotic' personalities.[28] This is a way of functioning that can also lead to breakdown at times of stress. Yet there are no absolute templates for emotional health, and thankfully the world is made up of a multitude of different personality types who cannot all be moulded into a therapist's idea of sanity. This is apparent in Donald Winnicott's concept of a true self,[29] and in the words of one Taoist sage who speaks of valuing people's differences: 'Fine horses can travel a hundred miles a day but they cannot catch mice.'

Getting it Off your Chest

'It makes me want to scream . . . may I? . . . Because that's maybe what I need most of all, to howl, a pure howl, without any words between me and it!

. . . Aaaaaaaaaaaaaaaaaaaaaaaaaaaaaaaaaaaaaaaaa
aaaaaaaaaaaaaaaaaaaaaaaaaaaaaaaahhhhh!!!!!' . . .
PUNCH LINE
'So' said the doctor. 'Now vee may perhaps to
begin. Yes?'[30]

(Philip Roth, *Portnoy's Complaint*)

Ray brought his son to a child guidance clinic complaining that the boy was out of control, and always getting into trouble. In explaining his son's emotional state he said that 'he has too much anger inside', that 'he has got to get it out'. The idea that we may have feelings inside that we need to get rid of is common, and is based on a view of emotions as being rather like bodily substances that we need to discharge. This is a kind of 'toxic waste model' of emotionality, in which the bad feelings will do us or someone else harm if allowed to remain inside. Freud's earliest therapeutic methods placed a similar emphasis on what was then called 'abreaction' or 'the cathartic method', and he found that symptoms did improve, albeit sometimes temporarily, when patients could experience and think about previously 'held in' or denied feelings.

This idea intuitively makes a lot of sense. *Ruby* seemed tense and stressed when her husband came home. She rushed around determinedly setting about household tasks and her whole body and musculature were taut, like a sprung coil. The phone rang and while answering it her manner was brusque and abrasive, brushing aside any enquiry as to how she was. She had been like this for a day and a half and her husband was concerned and perplexed. At first she held her husband at bay but when he presented her with a bunch of flowers her manner softened and she was surprised to find herself sobbing loudly as she allowed herself to be comforted by him. As Ruby relaxed she realised what had been going on. The flowers were what he knew to be her favourite colour chrysanthemums, and these were her favourite because her father would bring them home to her mother every Friday. On seeing them she felt a sudden overwhelming longing for her father, and realised that she was approaching the anniversary of his death.

From one angle we might say that she was carrying around feelings which she was only able to 'let out' on the receipt of her husband's gift. Another way of looking at this is that her husband helped her to manage and process feelings that she was warding off and possibly denying. Rather than getting rid of the feelings, she was in fact helped to have them. There are many forms of therapy ranging from 'primal scream' to 'encounter groups' which stress the need to express one's feelings, and it is the expression of emotionality and helping people to 'get in touch with their feelings' which is deemed therapeutic. Most current psychoanalytic therapists would come at this from a slightly different angle and think that it is the capacity for emotional understanding that is central. Sometimes we need help in processing and tolerating emotional experiences, something a mother often does for a child, and that a friend, spouse or therapist might do for an adult. The value of expressing feelings is not in just 'getting them out' but in expressing them to another. If we get something off our chest the feelings do not just fly off into the ether. What is helpful is having someone else, or a part of the self, who can listen to one's emotional state and help manage it.

In another example, a young child *Jessica* was angrily crashing around her bedroom. Her mother turned to her and said, 'yes, I understand, you are very very cross, you don't like it when daddy goes out at teatime, it just doesn't feel fair'. At this, the child calmed down and was able to talk about being angry and upset, and then sad, and eventually she was able to come down and eat her supper. What was important was having someone to help her to process and regulate her feelings.[31] It is to be hoped that in time we will all develop some capacity to process our emotional experiences, with or without the aid of others.

Throwing Stones from Glass Houses

. . . one should examine oneself for a very long time before thinking of condemning others.[32]

(Molière)

Some feelings are too much to bear; we do not want them and do our utmost to rid ourselves of them. A young woman *Martha* grew up feeling aggrieved that her younger brother was the favourite in the family. She responded by always being good, trying desperately to gain the respect and approval of her parents. She assumed it was her fault that her brother was preferred. As she grew up, Martha strove to assume the moral high ground and was quick to condemn any behaviour in others that she saw as immoral or wrong. She was surprisingly tuned in to any hint of unfairness and impropriety. Those around her often felt that they were not quite good enough, her women friends complaining that they always felt as if 'their slip was showing' when with her, and family, friends and colleagues felt tarnished, bad and generally in the wrong. Martha herself was not above acting in a fashion that others might call unscrupulous. She was pushy and tough at work, would tread on people's toes to get what she wanted and, oddly enough, people often felt rather let down by her. Yet Martha always seemed able to have a reason for her behaviour and would make those around her feel guilty and awkward if she were questioned. The more she acted in such a way, the more morally assertive she seemed to get, and if anyone else would challenge her they were firmly put in their place. Martha had never really felt good about herself, and she tried to manage this by getting rid of these self-hating feelings that she found so burdensome. She managed this in a twofold way, by trying to convince herself that it was others who were bad and had the problem, and also by trying to make sure that these others actually felt the bad feelings that she could not bear.

This process of disowning aspects of ourselves yet seeing these traits all too clearly in others is called *projection*.[33] The angry person who feels they should not be angry is all too quick to accuse others of being aggressive when stirred up. An adolescent who is insecure about their identity might be quick to denigrate and criticise another teenager for being 'uncool'. Feelings and emotional states that we cannot manage in ourselves we can place firmly 'out there' in others, in the hope that we do not have to face them in ourselves. This is sometimes purely a mental event, what psychoanalysis calls an 'intrapsychic' process. We see cruelty in others that we are quick to condemn, conveniently forgetting our own capacity to be cruel. Yet the condemnation might remain confined to our thoughts, having no effect on anyone else.

There is another version of getting rid of unwanted emotional states, which we also saw with Martha, and this has more effect on other people. *Patrick* is an inveterate Romeo, a young man who takes pleasure in seducing young women and then discarding them. He has left scores of hurt women in his all-conquering wake. None of his 'relationships' lasts more than a few days, after which he wriggles out of the situation and flees. It is interesting to question why he needs to do this. On meeting him, people seem to feel a need to please him and even a yearning to be liked by him, and women have often felt that they can be the one to save him from himself. Psychoanalysis might try to find some meaning in Patrick's seemingly compulsive behaviour. At one level, he actually believes that he is looking for a lasting relationship and is unhappy at their continual failures. Yet if we look a little closer, another story emerges. Patrick came from a difficult background: his mother was a heroin addict and he was taken into care when he was 3 years old. He lived with a series of foster families and children's homes until adolescence, when he remained with one foster family but was never adopted. He clearly did not have an ideal start in life, and his basic needs for intimacy and closeness had never been met. As an infant he had had glimpses of some genuine closeness with his mother, but she had sadly never been able to sustain these. Consequently he had experienced a tantalising promise of a loving if over-intense bond that seemed to be cruelly whisked away. It is no coincidence that his early experience, both of being offered the hope of safe loving closeness and of this hope being dashed, is the experience that his 'victims' undergo. A feeling that is unbearable is evacuated into someone else, so that the young women who fall for him suffer emotional states that he could not bear. Such ways of communicating can become ingrained and indeed can have their own secondary rewards. Patrick in fact learnt to enjoy the power that came with his conquests. Victims of abuse who then abuse others may start by trying to 'get rid of' feelings into others, but then begin to enjoy the power and control.

Getting rid of unbearable feelings is a common way of managing that which otherwise might seem unmanageable. We sometimes see these processes more clearly in young children. Six-year-old *Ben* had been teased and taunted by a boy in his street. He warded off the upset feelings but then went home and teased and bullied his younger brother who ended up feeling just what Ben did not want to feel. Ben could not manage his own feelings and got rid of them into his brother.

The young girl *Jessica* had been to her school open day and a high-achieving classmate subtly but somewhat cattily derided her artwork. Jessica left, feeling uncreative and rather dull, and it was no coincidence that later on, when provoked, she cuttingly attacked her parents' conservative taste in décor and style, accusing them of being bourgeois and unimaginative.

The ability to manage one's own emotional states rather than having to discharge them into others is taken by psychoanalysis as a sign of maturity. Life becomes much richer for the likes of Ben or Jessica when they can 'own' their upset feelings, rather than trying to get rid of them into others.

A common psychoanalytic model is that seen in parent–infant interactions. A distressed infant may try to relieve themselves of unbearable states of mind by, for example, kicking, screaming, crying or banging their head. A parent witnessing this will have all manner of feelings stirred up, and it is their role to make sense of these feelings. This is no easy matter. However, when successful, the parent might be able to receive the infant's communication and soothe and comfort them, making the situation bearable if not completely better.

Flooded by Feelings

Earlier I gave examples of people who seem 'cut off' from their feelings. An opposite problem confronts the person who is overwhelmed by feelings which they cannot control. *Janine* was the only child of a single mother who in turn had had a difficult upbringing. Janine's mother found parenting hard and managed by being emotionally absent and guiltily giving Janine what she wanted. As a child, Janine only had to threaten tears and her requests would be met – for sweets, new toys, her mother's attention and much else. As she grew up, Janine learnt that she could get what she wanted by making people feel guilty, having tantrums, making threats and by other manipulative means. She was someone who had never learnt how to manage frustration, nor to appreciate that others too have needs and feelings. She might fly off the handle when mildly challenged, or sulk, or storm off. She had few friends and people soon became wary of her. It seemed that she was flooded by feelings that she could not manage and would desperately get others to try to meet her needs. It is of course by no means only in women that we see such characters, and the male workplace bully or the abusive husband often shows a similar incapacity to manage his emotions, to the detriment of others. Such people cannot control their feelings. Rather, they are controlled *by* them. We might consider such people 'over-emotional', and indeed many such women are still pejoratively described as 'hysterical'. If we agree that such traits are by no means confined to women, then we might see some sense in the description one psychoanalyst made of the hysteric as 'a glass of water without the glass', seemingly raw emotion overflowing, with no modulating self that exists to withstand the torrential outflow of feeling states.[34]

Such people are described as 'brittle' or 'thin-skinned', unable to 'brush off' even petty slights and easily feeling hurt and upset, seeing criticism where it does not exist. As the academic Gillian Rose wrote movingly in her autobiographical fragment before she died:

. . . to grow in love-ability is to accept the

boundaries of oneself and others while remaining vulnerable, woundable, around the bounds.[35]

People who are more cut off from their feelings might be described as 'thick-skinned' rather than 'thin-skinned', some erecting a protective armour against emotional experiences they cannot tolerate. Defences can be set up to ward off painful feelings, such as engaging in manic activity or escaping into an intellectual retreat. In infancy the parent or primary caretaker tends to be an external regulator of a child's psychological life, what some have called a 'protective shield'. This is another way of saying that the emotional life of an infant is held together by the protective membrane of parental care. Such metaphors as 'skin' and 'membrane' and 'defences' and others such as 'fragility' or 'brittleness' describe something about how people develop very different methods of regulating their emotional lives. Janine is someone who cannot control her emotions and can be something of a 'loose cannon'. She shows little sense of a self in touch with her feelings. There is a seeming absence in place of a thoughtfulness or inner stillness. W. H. Auden writes of 'home' as an internal place:

A sort of honor, not a building site
Wherever we are, when if we choose, we might
Be somewhere else but trust that we have chosen
  right.[36]

Janine would seem to lack this. From another angle, Janine all too readily uses certain emotional responses to ward off or defend against other less tolerable ones. It is easier for her to feel anger than remorse, fury than anxiety, as she never developed the tools to manage these other kinds of feelings. Consequently she staves them off by jumping into well-trodden dramatic feeling states such as rage and self-pity. If Janine had been lucky enough to receive help in managing painful situations and tolerating frustration, her story might well have been different.

This way of understanding how one tolerates painful emotional experience links with trauma.

Trauma is a word used widely these days in the media and elsewhere. The word originally was a medical term meaning a serious wound or injury. A serious wound such as a bad head injury pierces the outer 'membrane' that protects the physiological system beneath. An emotional trauma is of a similar order. A working definition of a traumatic experience might be one that overwhelms one's ordinary emotional abilities. The starkest examples are the most unthinkable ones, such as surviving the Holocaust or being a victim of torture. The *unthinkability* of such experiences is often a sign of their traumatic nature, the experiences being too difficult to process.

Traumas can be of varying kinds and severity. *Peter* was riding home on his bike when he was attacked by a group of youths. He was beaten and his money and bicycle were stolen. Following a brief hospital admission, he could not leave home for a long period, had constant frightening flashbacks of the events, and suffered sleeplessness interrupted only by nightmares. He was extremely anxious, could not work and was not able to manage the life he had before. His experience was traumatic and he was showing all the common symptoms of what is now called *post-traumatic stress disorder*. One explanation of what happened to Peter is that he was overwhelmed by something that his emotional capacities could not manage, as would happen to many of us under those circumstances.

What is traumatic for one person might well affect another differently. For example, girls who have been sexually abused are more likely to make a better recovery if they have had good early emotional experiences. The severity of the abuse is not necessarily the main factor, and it is the help in processing emotional experiences, whether from a friend or from inside oneself, that counts for most. Some experiences, such as being in a concentration camp, would overwhelm just about anyone. My general theme has been that some people more than others develop the capacity to manage, modulate, process and generally experience a range of emotional states, often as a result of their early experiences. People tolerate different thresholds of emotional input, can be thrown off balance by different things, have different kinds of emotional 'skins' or 'membranes', and consequently need different kinds of help.

The Emotional Body

I wrote earlier that one could consider the 'site' of the emotions to be the body, whereas the 'site' of feelings might be the mind. Nowadays it is possible for scientists in laboratories to experimentally stimulate people to feel all manner of things and see the related response in the brain. Feelings have a bodily counterpart, whether in the brain or in signs such as shallow breathing when tense. There is a tendency in some circles to dismiss un-explained physical symptoms as 'all in the mind'. This is not an explanation in itself because often people have real physical symptoms, such as in phantom pregnancies, even if little sense can be made of them. Other physical ailments or disorders are sometimes described as being 'psychosomatic' or 'caused by stress'. A psychosomatic illness is often thought of as one which has an emotional as opposed to a physical cause. The word psycho-somatic can imply that the 'real' cause of the ailment is in someone's mind, and so wrongly suggest that the physical symptom is less than real. A danger that psychotherapists have to be aware of is omnipotently thinking that all physical symptoms can be explained psychologically.

Seeing the mind and body as separate entities is too simple, despite the fact that Western intellectual traditions going back to Descartes and before have tended to differentiate the mind or soul from the body. An emotion has a physical correlate, whether in the measurable responses in our neuronal pathways and synaptic connections, or in other physical manifestations. It is simpler to see them as two sides of the same coin. A feeling is the subjective aspect of what is physically observable as a bodily response. Upset, embarrassment, fear or anger all have physical correlates.

The baby Robert, mentioned earlier, who was so terrified at the sound of the tumble dryer, gave all kinds of signs of his fear and panic. Yet he did not know that what he was feeling was something called 'panic'. It took his mother to both alleviate his distress and to make sense of what he had been experiencing. There was nothing magical about what his mother did, as emotionally gruelling and difficult as her role is. Part of what she did was to read the signs from Robert's gestures and bodily state, and make sense of them. This is one way of saying that bodily states can be understood as signs or symptoms of psychological states. Robert will hopefully become someone who will be better than most at reading his own bodily signs.

There have been increasing links in recent years between psychoanalytic thinkers and researchers into psychosomatic states.[37] Most now agree that affects are initially experienced in one's body, as physiological states. These can gradually become what we might call subjective states – feelings or emotional experience – but the origin of such a sense of having feelings is 'intersubjective'. In other words, we initially need help to recognise that what is happening to us might be called an emotional state, such as upset or anger or sadness. Infants and children who do not receive such help may never move past the physiological sensations.

A few people have very little sense of an emotional life and seem flat, emotionless or detached. Such people, sometimes described as 'alexythmic', might dissociate from feelings they cannot manage, and are far more likely to suffer from what are called 'psychosomatic disorders'.[38] One interesting feature in such cases is that these people often have developed very little capacity for self-care or self-regulation, and thus are not very well able to look after themselves. These people are at a stage prior to either suppressing their emotions or projecting them into others, managing neither of these, and are barely off the starting blocks in terms of processing their emotional experience. In such cases, an impact which cannot be experienced psychologically might be said to reside in the body. Indeed, the research seems to illustrate what psychoanalytic thought has long argued, that psychosomatic symptoms are sometimes, if by no means always, an example of unprocessed emotional states 'lodged' in the body. This is the sense in statements such as 'the body never lies'. Our everyday language is replete with examples which hint at links between bodily and emotional states, such as 'feeling sick of' something, or someone being a 'pain in the neck', or 'making one's blood boil'.

Such people are extreme examples of something we all experience in varying degrees, which is an inability to work through an emotional state that threatens to overwhelm us, and the consequent effect of this in ailments or symptoms. Psychoanalysis has often fallen into the trap of explaining away real physical ailments as by-products of psychological states. Yet the emotional and the somatic *are* interlinked, related and joined in complex ways.

Get Happy

A wondrous portal opened
As if a cavern was suddenly hollowed
And the Pied Piper advanced
And the children followed.[39]

(Browning)

Psychoanalysis has been accused of being better at helping people to manage unhappiness than to become happier. Freud himself stated that the aim of psychoanalysis was to change human misery into 'ordinary unhappiness', and elsewhere that the hoped-for result of treatment is that people can manage to both love and work. These are real achievements, but some people feel that there is more to a good life. Psychoanalysis has helped in understanding how people defend against painful emotional realities, but perhaps has been less successful in thinking about what makes people happy. For many of us, even accepting compliments or praise is difficult. Often people manage to sabotage their own attempts at happiness, and also fear the risk of reaching out for what is really desired in case it will go wrong.

Martin met a woman, *Alison*, at a party and felt very attracted to her. They arranged to meet again and he was very excited. However, on this second date he was extremely nervous and was constantly searching for clues to prove that Alison was less keen on him than he on her. This made Martin tense and spoilt the evening so that he effectively made his worries come true. Martin had recently broken up with a long-term partner, which was a huge shock and blow to his confidence. It had stirred up feelings about his mother's departure from the family home when he was 7 years old. Indeed, he tended to think that if he got close to anyone, they would leave, and he could rarely dare to hope for and believe that things would work out well. Martin was rather like the doleful and morose Eeyore in *Winnie the Pooh*. Where others might see a cup half-full, Martin was a 'half-empty man', always looking on the dark side where others might see hope. Early on in his life, he had, for good reason, learned not to be complacent and not to trust what seemed good, because in his experience good things went wrong. But this was having a crippling effect on his life, not allowing him to make use of real opportunities for happier experiences. Whenever he had a hopeful idea, he always managed to come up with something to counter it, a worry or a fear, and inevitably the hope got quashed. As in the rhyme from the Ancient Mariner:

Fear at my heart, as at a cup
My life-blood seemed to sip.[40]

(S. T. Coleridge)

Martin lacked confidence, but this was about more than just confidence. He had developed a whole personality or character structure around being safe and not hoping for too much. Martin needed help to allow himself good feelings and not kill them off. Where Martin might see danger and start to worry, another person might see an opportunity, and it can take therapeutic help to begin to face life with hope and confidence. This requires a therapy which does not just aim to help people process painful experience, but also to manage happy and positive experiences.

Robert Frost describes the terrors of daring to desire in a poem appropriately called 'Peril of Hope':

It is right in there
Betwixt and between
The orchard bare

And the orchard green,

When the boughs are right
In a flowery burst
Of pink and white,
That we fear the worst.

For there's not a clime
But at any cost
Will take that time
For a night of frost.[41]

It is sometimes easier to see such traits developing in young children. Five-year-old *Stephanie* was out in the park with her father. She was trying to climb to the top of a very high climbing frame, and had started full of confidence. Now she was showing caution, and looking around for help as her confidence ebbed away. She was on the verge of giving up. Her father noticed and began to talk to her, saying 'yes, well done, you've done really well, it is scary up there, but I think you can do it, yes, there you go, three more steps, yes just two more now, nearly there, what a brave girl, yes you can do it, well done'. It was fascinating to watch how Stephanie responded. Taking courage from her father, she found new resources and succeeded where she had believed she would fail. The ensuing smile of pleasure, and look of triumph and achievement, was delightful. Children very quickly learn from such experiences and can build up an expectation that they can achieve things, that situations can go well, and that they can dare to have hopes. Courage and hope are neglected emotions in psychoanalysis, as are other positive affects. The baby whose beaming smile is met with a responsive mirroring grin, whose efforts to reach out and play are reciprocated, is likely to begin to feel that they can have an impact on the world and that their wishes can come true.

The child who is constantly judged, criticised or ignored will not have such confidence, such a sense of their own abilities, or belief that they can make a difference. The neglected child can easily give up trying and retreat into his or her own world. The parent who is constantly criticising and carping is likely to have an adverse impact on the confidence of a child like Stephanie. Psycho-analysts have helpfully talked about people maintaining defences against tolerating emotional pain, but it can also be true that defences are erected against taking in good, hopeful or loving experiences. Depression and upset can be clung to, often with the belief that it is 'better the devil you know'. Sticking to that with which we are familiar, even if it makes us unhappy, is at least safe and is often easier than risking change, and so also risking failing to be able to change and the consequent disappointments of such a failure.

Many psychotherapists, particularly those who work with children, have come to realise that when some children or adults are being tough or boastful or over-exuberant, they are not always defending against painful feelings. Sometimes they are, and then they need help to tolerate an un-palatable reality. Others, though, have lacked the good early experiences many take for granted. *Sheila* was a 16-year-old who had been in the care system for most of her life. When she arrived for therapy she would spend a lot of time denigrating others in a rather desperate attempt to bolster her flimsy sense of self. However, in time she slowly made some real progress and achievement and there was a subtle but definite change in the manner in which she would 'talk herself up'. It was important that the therapist did not confuse the two kinds of self-assertion, and that her real if precarious achievements were openly validated and acknowledged. Every child at times benefits from feeling that they 'are king of the castle', as long as it is a genuine trying out of the feeling of being special and not desperately trying to make someone else feel bad, or bolstering up a false good sense of themselves.[42]

We need to be able to experience joy and exuberance on the one hand, pain and difficulty on the other, and all that comes in between. An old rabbinic saying goes that a man should have two pockets into which he can reach. In the one should be the words 'for my sake was the world created', and in the other 'I am dust and ashes'.[43]

Positive feelings have received a bad press within psychoanalysis and psychoanalysis has received its own bad press as a result. Within some psycho-analytic circles this is changing somewhat, as an acknowledgement has grown of the need to be aware of and work with positive emotional states as well. Much as we would hope that people, through a psychoanalytic therapy, can develop a greater capacity to tolerate and manage the painful things in life, so we would also hope that people can develop the psychological tools and abilities to genuinely enjoy life at times and take the risk of courageously reaching out for what they had too often thought was beyond their grasp. Once again I have emphasised that what is important is to develop the tools and capacities to manage a broad range of affective experience, positive and nega-tive, to be able to actively allow and enjoy such emotional states in oneself, and to be empathetic to them in others.

Conclusions

Midway along the journey of our life
I ... found myself within a gloomy wood.

So hard it is its aspects to describe,
This savage, harsh and fearsome wilderness,
That fear rekindles with the memory . . .
Yet to recall the good that came of it
I shall set forth all else I there beheld. [44]

(Dante, *Inferno*)

Affect is central to psychoanalysis and is indissolubly linked with it. A psychoanalytic perspective is unique in emphasising the centrality of unconscious processes, and how specific unconscious mental and affective constellations and processes have a profound impact on who we are and how we act. Denying feelings and projecting are two ways in which painful experiences may be defended against, just as dreams, slips of the tongue, free association and creative pursuits may unwittingly reveal such unconscious affective processes.

People possess different capacities to process and manage emotional experience which otherwise may be dealt with in less satisfactory ways. An abundance of developmental research has been published in recent years that stresses the importance of learning to regulate one's emotional life. The work also shows how the roots of this learning lie firmly in early childhood and in having a good experience of one's emotions being thought about, regulated and understood. The capacity for self-care, for understanding our own feelings and for reflecting on our emotional lives, will only develop, assuming that there are no organic problems, if one's emotions have been thoughtfully reflected upon by another.

Emotional understanding is vastly different from simply 'knowing about' something in a cognitive or intellectual way. Emotional knowledge is *visceral*, held within procedural memories which are deeply ingrained in our bodies and personalities. Expectations of how social interactions are likely to go are laid down early in life and become unconscious and as natural to us as driving a car or tying a shoelace. The therapeutic task is partly to make sense of these emotional patterns as they arise in therapy, often in relation to a therapist or analyst. The distrustful person is likely to show profound distrust of their therapist, just as the person who needs to please others will try to be the best patient. Hopefully, old patterns can be understood and new patterns emerge, as new trains of associations – new networks of neuronal pathways – are set in motion. This is never solely an intellectual process, but a profoundly emotional one also, often fraught with discomfort and anxiety as well as, hopefully, relief.

Self-reflection – thinking about and processing feelings – plays a central part in this. The idea of self-reflection presupposes a self that can self-reflect; some, like the 'thin-skinned' characters mentioned earlier, have little sense of their own self. Again, extensive research has shown that certain kinds of parents are far more likely to have children who are described as 'securely attached' than others. These parents are the ones who are able to put together a coherent story about their own childhood experiences, without inconsistencies, without getting too emotional in their descriptions, but also without seeming to deny emotionally-laden experiences. These people have what is sometimes called a capacity for 'self-reflexivity', that has also been called the capacity to 'mentalise',[45] or in other words to reflect upon their emotional experience. Such people are much more likely to be able to give a similar quality of thoughtful emotional understanding to their own children. This is a similar type of attention to that which one would hope psychotherapists might be able to give to their patients. Some have argued that psychoanalysis and its related therapies are unique in being the only form of therapy that aims to foster and develop this capacity for self-reflection, for making sense of and reflecting upon the emotional vagaries that life throws up. Such a therapy does not beget someone who fully understands their unconscious, nor someone who has control of their emotional life. However, it might result in people better able to read signs of unconscious processes, and better able to tolerate and experience a genuine depth and breadth in their emotional lives, better able to manage the vicissitudes of intimacy, of pain, of joy and equally of the mundane, and whose lives will be considerably richer as a result.

Notes

1. W. Wordsworth, 'The Prelude' (1850), II.ii.401–5 in *The Prelude*. Harmondsworth: Penguin Books, 1971.

2. For a more complex discussion from another angle see I. Matthis, 'Sketch for a Metapsychology of Affect', in *International Journal of Psychoanalysis*, vol. 81, part 2, 2000.

3. J. Updike, *Rabbit is Rich,* New York: Knopf, 1981.

4. A. Damasio, *The Feeling of What Happens*, London: Heinemann, 1999.

5. S. Greenfield, *Brain Power,* London: Element, 2000.

6. This experiment and linked research by various people is reported in e.g. B. Beebe, F. Lachmann and J. Jaffe, 'Mother-infant Interaction Structures', in *Psychoanalytic Dialogues*, vol. 7, no. 2, 1997.

7. Quoted in P. Cousineau (ed.), *The Soul of the World*, San Francisco: Harper, 1993.

8. R. W. Emerson, 'Worship' (1860), in *Conduct of Life,* in *The Collected Works of R.W. Emerson*, London: Harvard University Press, 1987.

9. W. Shakespeare, *Richard III*, E. A. Honigmann and T. J. B. Spencer (eds), London: Penguin, 1981.

10. M. Buber, *Tales of the Hassidim* (1966), New York: Schocken Books, quoted in S. B. Kopp, *Guru*, California: SBB, 1971. Emphasis added.

11. Ibid.

12. V. Brittain, *The Testament of Youth* (1933), Glasgow: William Collins, 1978, p. 247.

13. T. Hardy, 'In Tenebris II' (1928), in *Collected Poems,* London: Macmillan, 2000.

14. Melanie Klein and those who have developed her tradition have written extensively about 'internal objects'.

15. H. Beecher Stowe, *Uncle Tom's Cabin* (1852), New York: Chelsea House, 1996.

16. S. Plath, 'You're' (1960), in T. Hughes (ed.), *Collected Poems*, London: Faber and Faber, 1981, p. 141.

17. B. Beebe et al., op. cit.

18. J. Bowlby, *Attachment and Loss,* New York: Basic Books, 1980.

19. D. N. Stern, *The Interpersonal World of the Infant*, New York: Basic Books, 1984, particularly chapters 4 and 5.

20. A. Schore, *Affect Regulation and the Origin of the Self*, Hillsdale, NJ: Erlbaum, 1994.

21. B. Perry, R. A. Pollard, T. L. Blackley, W. L. Baker and D. Vigilante, 'Childhood Trauma, the neurobiology of adaptation and the use-dependent development of the brain, how states become traits', in *Infant Mental Health Journal*, 16(4), 1950.

22. D. H. Lawrence, *Sex, literature and censorship*, London: Heinemann, 1955.

23. B. Keenan, *An Evil Cradling*, London: Vintage, 1992, p. 261.

24. R. Horrocks, *Male Myths and Icons*, London: Macmillan, 1995.

25. Eva Hoffman, *Lost in Translation*, London: Vintage, 1998, p. 29.

26. B. Beebe, op. cit.

27. J. McDougall, *Plea for a Measure of Abnormality*, London: Free Association Books, 1990.

28. C. Bollas, *The Shadow of the Object*, London: Free Association Books, 1987.

29. D. W. Winnicott, *The Maturational Process and the Facilitating Environment*, London: Karnac, 1965.

30. P. Roth, *Portnoy's Complaint*, London: Penguin Books, 1969.

31. W. R. Bion developed the theory of 'containment' to explain this capacity, particularly in W. R. Bion, *Learning from Experience*, London: Heinemann, 1962.

32. Molière, *The Doctor in Spite of Himself* (*Le Médecin Malgré Lui*, 1666–7), III.iv, London: Applause Books, 1997.

33. The linked concept of projective identification has been developed by Melanie Klein and her followers. See, for example, M. Klein, 'Notes on some schizoid mechanisms' (1946), in *The Writings of Melanie Klein*, London: Hogarth Press and the Institute of Psycho-

analysis, 1975. Also, H. Racker, *Transference and Countertransference*, London: Hogarth Press, 1968.

34. P. Bromberg, *Standing in the Spaces,* New Jersey: Analytic Press, 1998.

35. G. Rose, *Love's Work*, London: Vintage, 1997, p. 98.

36. W. H. Auden, 'In War Time' (1942), quoted in P. Gordon, *Face to Face*, London: Constable, 1999, chapter 5, in which this theme is developed. This poem does not appear in current collections of Auden's work.

37. L. Aron and F. S. Anderson (eds), *Relational Perspectives on the Body*, New Jersey: Analytic Press, 1998.

38. J. McDougall, *Theatres of the Body,* London: Free Association Books, 1989.

39. R. Browning, *The Pied Piper* (1888), London: Orchard Books, 1994.

40. S. T. Coleridge, 'The Rime of the Ancient Mariner', in *The Collected Works of Samuel Taylor Coleridge,* London: Dover Publications, 1992.

41. R. Frost, 'Peril of Hope' (1962), in *Selected Poems,* London: Penguin, 1973, p. 226.

42. A. Alvarez, *Live Company,* London: Routledge, 1992.

43. Quoted in S.B. Kopp, *Guru*, California: SBB, 1971.

44. Dante Alighieri, *The Inferno*, New York: Thames and Hudson, 1985.

45. These ideas have been explored by Peter Fonagy, for example: P. Fonagy and M. Target, 'Mentalization and the changing Aims in Child Psychoanalysis', *Psychoanalytic Dialogues*, 8, 1998, pp. 87–114.

Dedication

For Sue and Rose

Acknowledgements

With thanks to Ivan Ward and all at Icon Books for their patience and support. For encouragement, candid comments and lively discussions and inspiration, thank you to Anne Alvarez, Melissa Benn, Dilys Daws, Robert Glanz, Paul Gordon, Mary-Pat O'Gorman, Helen Wright, and last but most, Sue Beecraft.